Mary Throughout Latin America

A REDEMPTORIST PASTORAL PUBLICATION

LIGUORI

LIGUORI, MISSOURI

Imprimi Potest:
Thomas D. Picton, C.Ss.R.
Provincial, Denver Province
The Redemptorists

Published by Liguori Publications
Liguori, Missouri
www.liguori.org

Library of Congress Cataloging-in-Publication Data

[María en Latinoamérica. English]
Mary throughout Latin America / compiled and edited by Daniel T. Michaels ; introduction and prayers by Mathew Kessler, C.Ss.R.–1st ed.

     p. cm. (A Redemptorist pastoral publication)
   ISBN 0-7648-1224-6 (pbk.)
   1. Mary, Blessed Virgin, Saint—Devotion to—Latin America.

BT652.91'098–dc 22   2005040933

The publisher gratefully acknowledges the Marian Library/International Marian Research Institute at the University of Dayton for the use of the images throughout this book.

Liguori Publications, a nonprofit corporation, is an apostolate of the Redemptorists. To learn more about the Redemptorists, visit *Redemptorists.com*.

Printed in Mexico
09 08 07 06 05   5 4 3 2 1
First edition

Liguori Publications wishes to express thanks to South-east Regional Office for Hispanic Ministry, Inc. (SEPI) for permission to use Las Advocaciones Marianas en la Religiosidad Popular Latinoamericana, *which formed the basis of this work.*

Contents

Mary, our Mother,
strengthen and enliven our hearts
to embrace the Christian journey
with the same conviction and spirit
as the testimonies of faith herein.

Introduction

You have made us for yourself, O Lord,
and our hearts are restless until they rest in you.
SAINT AUGUSTINE

With Saint Augustine, holy men and women throughout the ages have counseled Christians to listen attentively to the restlessness of their hearts. Christians interpret this spiritual agitation as the beginning of the journey to know God, the source of our deepest longings. Along the way, we look for encouragement: A hand to lead us back to the correct path or a shoulder to lean on when the road becomes steep and failure seems unavoidable. Traditionally, Catholics—particularly Latinos—turn to the Blessed Virgin to calm their spirits and guide them on the path toward God.

The Church rejoices that Mary is known in all cultures of the world, and that her maternal qualities provide a concrete expression of God's tender mercy. For many people Mary's quiet, strong presence is essential for overcoming the ignorance, hatred, injustice, and violence that stand in the way of the kingdom of God. For Latinos—indeed, for all people—consolation and encouragement are found in the woman who holds an infant in her arm or who refuses to leave a special spot near a natural spring or river.

The brief passages of this book record the stories and images of Latino witnesses to the loving guidance of Mary. They provide an account of the actions of God's blessing; encouraging, protecting, and inspiring women and men to believe that their turbulent lives can find the peace that only Jesus brings. Mary's life, as it is expressed through the people of God, is proof that the Lord is close to us no matter what language we speak or which continent we call home.

Our Lady of Luján

Our Lady of Luján, a fifteen-inch terra cotta figure, is modeled after an image of the Immaculate Conception. She is adorned with a crown and draped with an ornate white alb and rich sky-blue cape intended to mimic the national colors of Argentina. She prayerfully stands in front of a blue mandorla, the symbolic union of heaven and earth.

MAY 8 According to legend, the statue was shipped from Buenos Aires to Santiago del Estero along with another figure of the Virgin holding the Child Jesus in 1630. The Marian duo was placed into an ox-drawn wagon amid many other transported goods. En route from Buenos Aires to Santiago del Estero, the oxen inexplicably stopped by the Luján River. Fearing exhaustion from the overloaded wagon, the merchants rotated the oxen, readjusted the goods, and rested for the evening. Nevertheless, even the refreshed animals refused to carry the load. As the merchants continued to invent new ways to reactivate the transport, one of them removed the statue of the Immaculate and the oxen immediately began moving. Astonished witnesses observed again and again how the cart stopped every time the statue was placed back onto it. Clearly, Our Lady wished to remain in Luján.

The presence of this miraculous symbol prompted great devotion and the construction of a shrine in Luján, where Our Lady continues to bless the faithful. As a testament to their faith, Pope Leo XII (1887) blessed the image and later Pope Pius XI (1930) elevated the shrine to the status of basilica.

Prayer

Our Lady of Luján,

as a sign of your maternal

protection of the people of

Argentina, an image of the

Immaculate Conception

was miraculously sent

to your people.

Help us to break the

barriers of sin so that,

like you,

we may fold our hands

and unfold our hearts

to receive your son.

Amen.

Our Lady of Copacabana

This statue of the Blessed Virgin stands just over four feet in height and was formed from a combination of Bolivian maguey trees and plaster. Her garments mimic the color and dress of an Inca princess, with ornate patterns of gold leaf to accent her magnificence. Her gentle aura and the peaceful child in her arms—whose hand blesses onlookers even if he appears to fall—also reflect the inhabitants of the region.

AUGUST 5 This figure was crafted by Francisco Tito Yupanqui around 1583 near the sacred Incan islands of the sun and the moon. As a native of Bolivia, Francisco envisioned Our Lady with local features, thereby providing access to her motherly love for the faithful poor who prayed by her side. She inspired such devotion that over the centuries she acquired rich jewels and gifts, even attracting—for better or worse—the attention of local, national, and international rulers. The Quechuas and Aimaraes Indians call her "Queen of the Incas," and she is known to the Americas as the patroness of Bolivia.

As one of the oldest Marian shrines in the Western Hemisphere, Our Lady of Copacabana continues to adorn visitors inside a church formed in her honor. She was formally crowned by Pope Pius XI in 1925 and the church was promoted to a basilica in 1949.

Prayer

Our Lady of Copacabana—

our candle, our light—

you gave humanity the gift

of eternal salvation.

As the dreams of Simeon,

who hoped to see the

Messiah, were fulfilled,

complete in us the work

of your grace.

May we look to Christ

in this life,

and contemplate

his presence in eternity.

Amen.

Our Lady
of Aparecida

This deep-brown terra cotta sculpture lost its original multicolored appearance in the waters of the Paraiba River where she was discovered by fisherman. She stands about fifteen inches and wears a mantle of elegantly embroidered cloth that allows her adoring vision and clasped hands to be viewed. The fringes of her garment, and the jeweled imperial crown on her head, signify her role as patroness of Brazil.

OCTOBER 12 The legend of Aparecída originated with a series of events surrounding a visit to the people of Guarantinqueta by the Count of Assumar in 1717. In preparation for a great feast, three fisherman set out to gather the main course, despite the fact that the fishing season was over and the waters appeared deserted. After many hours with empty nets, the three men prayed to their heavenly Mother for assistance. To their surprise, they netted a statue of the Immaculate Conception. They decided to dedicate the remainder of their labor to the Virgin who appeared (*Aparecída*) and, not surprisingly, their nets were filled with fish.

After the miraculous discovery and a feast in honor of the Count of Assumar, one of the fisherman took the statue home and built a small shrine. By 1743 the community rallied around the image and erected a church in her honor.

The importance of this miraculous statue has been certified by Pope Pius XI who proclaimed her the patroness of Brazil in 1930 and Pope John Paul II who elevated the sanctuary to the level of basilica in 1980.

Prayer

Blessed Mary of Aparecida, we consecrate to you our thoughts, so that we may remember you; we consecrate to you our tongues, so that we may spread your devotion; we consecrate to you our hearts, so that, after God, we may love you above all things. Bless us, O Celestial Mother, that under your guidance, we may be fishers for God. *Amen.*

Our Lady of Carmen of Maipú

This statue of the Virgin of Mount Carmel (*Carmen* in Spanish) is dressed like the ancient Carmelites of the Holy Land: She wears the garments of religious life, colored in brown and tan, and she cradles the Infant Jesus in one arm. With her son, she holds a scapular, which is a traditional Carmelite necklace that has two holy prints and brown cloth encased in plastic.

JULY 16 Our Lady of Maipú was introduced to Chile in 1785 when Don Martin de Lecuna commissioned a sculptor from Quito, Ecuador, to portray Our Lady of Mount Carmel for the Chilean people. Like the reformers of the Carmelite Order from centuries past, they entrusted their lives to Mary as they fought and won their independence as a nation.

In honor of her protection, they celebrated a solemn Mass of thanksgiving in 1811. In 1817 she was adorned with a baton and proclaimed by the armies of the Andes as their formal patroness. In 1818, as Spanish forces descended upon the capital city of Santiago, the people and their leaders crowded into the cathedral to renew their pledge of trust in Mary and promised to erect a shrine on the spot in Maipú where Chile gained its independence. The original structure was completed in 1892.

In 1923 the Vatican named her the patroness of all Chileans. She is venerated through two depictions: one at the National Shrine of Maipú which was made in Quito, Ecuador, and another made in France and housed at the Basilica of the Savior in Santiago de Chile.

Prayer

Lady of Carmen,

your Chilean sons and

daughters rejoice to have

you as protector,

mother, and queen

of their country.

May harmony and justice,

and their fruits of peace

and prosperity,

flourish in our lives.

Amen.

15

Our Lady of the Rosary of Chinquinquirá

This beautiful fifty-by-forty-eight-inch Madonna was painted onto handwoven cotton with tempera created from soil and plant extracts. As if walking on an elevated crescent moon, she displays a rare smile as she cradles Jesus in her left arm. In contrast to her clothing and the two saints which flank her to the left and right (not pictured), her face and the Child's radiate with light. True to her given title, she carries the rosary in imitation of the Child who also offers one in his left hand.

JULY 9 The Spanish painter Alonso de Narvaez painted the image of Our Lady of the Rosary in 1562 for use in a small house chapel. The rustic environment of the painting obscured the image, fading its vibrant colors with humidity and sun damage. Fifteen years later the deteriorating image was placed into a storage room connected to a chapel in Chinquinquirá. In 1585, more than twenty years after its creation, the painting once again adorned the walls of a chapel due to the devotion of a woman from Seville who entrusted the oratory to her care. According to legend, on December 26, 1586, the Madonna, who held the woman's devotion, reemerged as if new; her colors brilliant, holes mended, displaying the Christ Child and rosary.

For centuries pious pilgrims have brushed religious objects against it in order to restore—like the image itself—the damaged and suffering parts of their lives. Our Lady's simple and loving response to the faithful was officially confirmed by Pope Pius VII when he declared her the patroness of Colombia and granted her a special liturgy. She was canonically crowned in 1915 and the sanctuary in her honor was elevated to the status of basilica in 1927.

Prayer

Lady of the Rosary,

you have favored Colombia

by giving a sign of your

presence in Chinquinquirá.

Through your intercession,

may we grow

in the ways of faith

and promote social

progress through

peace and justice.

Amen.

Our Lady of the Angels

Our Lady of the Angels—also known as *La Negrita*, the "Little Black One"—is a three-inch delicate dark-stone statuette. She has a soft, welcoming presence, accented by indigenous eyes and a delicate mouth. Her dark color stands in contrast to the gold and pleated cloak that cover all but the faces of her and the Christ Child. She is supported by a large gold monstrance held up by lilies (the Christian symbol of purity) and an angel.

AUGUST 2 According to tradition, on August 2, 1635, on the feast of Holy Angels, a poor Mestizo woman discovered the stone treasure of Mary alongside a footpath. She brought the statue home and it was quickly misplaced. Fearing its permanent loss, she returned to its point of origin where, to her surprise, she rediscovered the same statue in the same spot. She repeated this cycle many times—even taking it for safekeeping at the local church—but the Marian image always found its way back to the site where it was discovered. The community interpreted this miraculous relocation to identify the place for a new shrine.

Reminding the poor and afflicted of God's healing presence at this spot, a spring of water appeared from beneath the statuette, and thus reconfirmed the initiative for the construction of the shrine. The church quickly became a major pilgrimage site. By 1926 the original statuette was crowned and in 1935 Pope Pius XI raised the church to the level of basilica, and ever since people have continued to receive the blessed water and the healing presence of Our Lady of the Angels.

Prayer

Blessed Mother,

among the people

of Costa Rica,

you were welcomed

as Our Lady of the Angels.

May we persevere in

announcing the message

of your Son,

and never hesitate

to turn to you

for assurance in times

of distress.

Amen.

Our Lady of Charity of El Cobre

This sixteen-inch statue portrays Our Lady holding a cross in her right hand and the Infant Jesus in her left. The Child cradles a globe in his left hand while his right hand instills confidence in Mary with a blessing for the faithful. The head of the statue is made of clay and polished with paste in order to accent her delicate features. Her large and gentle eyes invite the viewer to trust in her intercession. She stands on a brilliant moon that is enveloped by a silver cloud and three golden cherubs.

SEPTEMBER 8

Between 1612 and 1613 two Cubans and a young Spaniard were gathering salt in the Bay of Nipe for use in the meat houses of El Cobre, when they noticed a white birdlike object sitting on dry palms. As they drew near, they realized that it was actually a statue of the Blessed Virgin. The statue was attached to a board on which was inscribed, "I am the Virgin of Charity." Despite unrest in the sea, neither the figure of Mary nor her clothing were wet.

The statue was taken to Barajagua for use in a local hermitage. According to legend, the image periodically disappeared for many hours at a time. After several such relocations, the statue was taken to the local parish in El Cobre, where it remained for nearly three years. But it continued to disappear and reappear from time to time. One day a young girl saw the image on the peak of a hill at a local copper mine. The community interpreted it as the location to which Our Lady had been disappearing. The statue was moved to the new site and a shrine was built in her honor.

Our Lady of Charity was named the patroness of Cuba by Pope Benedict XV in 1916, she was crowned the queen and protector of Cuba by Pope Pius XI in 1936, and Pope Paul VI elevated the sanctuary to a basilica in 1977.

Prayer

Our Lady of Charity,

we joyfully venerate you

as patroness of Cuba.

May we boldly take your

name and message

to the world,

so that the Gospel

will be announced

to all men and women.

Amen.

Our Lady of Altagracia

This thirteen-inch wide by eighteen-inch high painting on fine cloth portrays the Nativity of Jesus. The crowned Virgin is adorned with a deep-blue cloak and stars to indicate her universal appeal. With a gesture of prayer, she looks lovingly at the newborn Child resting on the straw of the manger. The work is believed to be the primitive work of a Spanish school painted towards the end of the fifteenth or beginning of the sixteenth century.

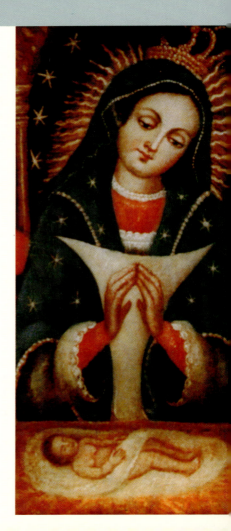

JANUARY 21 This painting dates back to the early evangelization of the Dominican Republic when Spanish colonials identified Mary as their protector under two titles: Our Lady of Mercy, the patroness of the country, and Our Lady of Altagracia ("full of grace") as the protector and queen of the Dominicans. Natives from the region of Quisqueya honored Our Lady of Altagracia through a portrait brought from Spain by the first European settlers of the island. The image was later brought to Higuey, where a shrine was constructed in 1572.

According to legend, a rich merchant sought the painting to assist the pious devotion of his daughter, who requested the image under that title. After a long and difficult search, he shared the story of his unsuccessful hunt with his friends. A man gave him a small piece of linen telling him, "This is what you are looking for." The next morning the man was nowhere to be found, and the father discovered that the linen gift was a beautiful depiction of Our Lady of Altagracia.

Our Lady of Altagracia has been crowned twice in order to recognize her role as the first evangelizer of the Americas: August 15, 1922, by Pope Pius XI, and on January 25, 1979, by Pope John Paul II.

Prayer

Blessed Virgin,

you are the Mother

of the Holy Family

and Mother of the Church.

Under the title of

Altagracia, may the

Dominican Republic

and all who dwell

in the world

experience your Son's

constant friendship.

Amen.

Our Lady of the Presentation of Quinché

This cedar wood sculpture stands just over two feet tall. Most of its delicate indigenous features are hidden beneath jeweled garments, but the serene faces of Mary and Jesus appear crowned with gold. The Virgin holds a scepter in her right hand, while holding the Child in her left. In a pose of benediction, the Child carries a golden globe crowned with a cross to signify his dominion over the world.

NOVEMBER 21 Our Lady of the Presentation of Quinché was carved by the famous artist, Don Diego de Robles, in the sixteenth century. This work was originally commissioned as Our Lady of the Presentation, but the patron was unable to pay for the sculpture so the artist traded it to the Oyacachi tribe in exchange for several more boards of cedar.

Legend has it that the Virgin appeared earlier to the Indians to offer her protection against the local bears that threatened their young children. Upon seeing the statue from Don Diego, they immediately recognized it as the exact replica of their vision. They cared for Our Lady for fifteen years, until her impact became too great for the small tribe to manage. The bishop had her moved to Quinché in 1604 and a shrine was built in her honor.

Owing to her native mestizo gentleness—dark color, soft eyes, and delicate bone structure—this image of Mary is one of Ecuador's most popular devotions, particularly among Indians who refer to her as *La Pequehita* ("The Little One").

The statue was not formally crowned until 1943, and the present shrine was officially declared a national sanctuary in 1985.

Prayer

Blessed Mother,

in the image

of your Presentation,

the people of Ecuador

find great security.

Grant that we,

with your assistance,

may be free from all evil

and become temples

of your glory.

Amen.

Our Lady of Peace

This wood statue of the Virgin is adorned with a white robe that has the national shield of El Salvador embroidered on the front. She carries Jesus in her left hand and a gold palm leaf in her right in memory of her intercession against a volcano that once threatened the city. Her indigenous facial features express peace and confidence.

NOVEMBER 21

The artist and origin of Our Lady of Peace remains somewhat mysterious. Hidden in a sealed box, she washed ashore on the Mar del Sur and was discovered by local merchants in 1682. They were unable to open the box and assumed that it contained precious treasure. They decided to take it to San Miguel where they could prove to authorities that it was discovered unopened, and perhaps they would be considered the rightful owners. Upon entering the city they passed by the church of San Miguel, when suddenly their mule sat down on the ground and refused to move. Only then were they able to open the box and discover the statue of the Virgin.

At the time of its discovery, there was much unrest in El Salvador. But the mysterious appearance of this image inspired enemies to put down their weapons in peace. The people vowed to abandon their grudges and to remove all hatred from their hearts. Thus the image was named Our Lady of Peace.

Our Lady of Peace was crowned by Pope Benedict XV in 1921 and a new shrine was completed in her honor in 1953.

Prayer

Our Lady of Peace,
you were with the sons
and daughters of
El Salvador as they
fought for peace.
You did not abandon them
when threatened
by natural disasters.
We pray that all countries
experience your Son's deep
eternal peace.

Amen.

Our Lady of the Rosary

This beautiful statue is made of pure silver—including robes and pedestal—and covered with ornate garments and jewels. Mary holds a large rosary in her right hand and the Infant Jesus—who appears to be sleeping—in her left. According to legend, her delicate face changes from a rose color to pale white as an indicator of the immanent fortune or misfortune for the nation.

OCTOBER 7 Although the artist is unknown, the image of Our Lady of the Rosary was commissioned by Lopez de Montoya, a Dominican priest, in 1592. The inspiration for the image came from a popular legend of the Virgin Mary traveling throughout Latin America. When she reached Guatemala, the Child fell asleep, and so Mary decided to remain. She quickly became a symbol of national pride and devotion. Her patronage was so significant that, in 1821, the leaders of an independence movement vowed that under her protection they would not rest until Guatemala was free, and afterward they named her the patroness of the new country.

Since the rosary plays such a central role in the image, the faithful devote October—the month of the rosary—to celebrating the Virgin and her role in their freedom with feasts and pilgrimages to her sanctuary.

The Shrine of the Virgin of the Rosary was completed in 1808, and Our Lady was solemnly declared "Queen of Guatemala" in 1833. She was officially recognized by Pope Pius XI in 1934 when he crowned her with precious metals and jewels and gave her shrine an apostolic blessing.

Prayer

Our Lady of the Rosary,

you and Jesus found rest

and a home among

the women and men

of Guatemala.

We ask your help

to remain free from all evil

and rest one day

in the eternal joy

of heaven.

Amen.

Our Lady of Suyapa

This delicate cedar wood statue is only about two and one-half inches tall. Although covered with an ornate cloak, Our Lady's facial features reveal her indigenous humility, with brown skin, large eyes, rounded cheeks, and shoulder-length dark hair. She stands with her hands folded in prayer (under her cloak) and she is crowned like a queen inside of a precious monstrance made of two radiant arcs that come together in the shape of an eight.

FEBRUARY 3 Our Lady has often chosen to appear to simple, humble, down-to-earth people, an indication of God's special love for the poor and afflicted. The statue of Our Lady of the Conception of Suyapa was discovered by an eight-year-old peasant boy in 1747 when he was returning from his work in the fields. His journey was long, so he stopped for the night on the hard open ground at the Pilígüin ravine. As he stretched out to sleep, he felt a sharp object poking his back. Thinking it was a stone, he cast it aside and returned to his slumber. However, as soon as he tried to sleep he felt the same object pressing against his back. With much curiosity he placed the object in his sack until daylight. That morning he discovered the cedar wood figure of the Virgin.

The shrine of Our Lady of Suyapa was consecrated in 1780, and the first recorded miracle occurred in 1796. To this day the enormous church draws pilgrims to one of the poorest regions of the land. In recognition for humble faith surrounding this devotion, Pope Pius XI declared Our Lady of Suyapa patroness of the Republic of Honduras in 1925, and Pope John Paul II visited the site in 1983.

Prayer

Virgin Mary,

as mother and queen

of the Republic

of Honduras,

many have found solace

in your constant presence.

Through your intercession

as Our Lady of Suyapa,

may we see others as true

brothers and sisters.

Amen.

Our Lady of Guadalupe

The famous image of Our Lady of Guadalupe was created on coarse cloth made from maguey fibers and measures 66 by 41 inches. In a delicate prayerful pose, with her face leaning slightly to the right, Our Lady is covered with a turquoise cloak that has stars evenly spaced throughout—an indication of her noble status in the community. The lines of her clothing and the black bow around her waist are indications that she is expecting. She stands on a black moon and is supported by an angel in full flight.

DECEMBER 12

On December 9, 1531, the Blessed Virgin appeared to Juan Diego, a native of Cuauhtilán, while he was on the way to Mass. Unaware of her identity, he had conversations with her for several days on the hill of Tepeyac. She asked him to request that the bishop build a chapel on the site of the apparition. From there she would listen to the plight of the people, and offer her "help and defense."

Juan was rejected by the bishop, but was asked to bring a sign of the apparitions. He returned shortly thereafter with an image of the Virgin stamped onto his *ayate*, a course cloth used to carry things. Upon this sign, the bishop constructed the chapel.

It took more than four hundred years before modern society realized the miraculous quality of the cloth. Over the years it was exposed to the rigors of the weather and continuous contact with pilgrims, yet this particular cloth—which normally only lasts twenty years—has persisted through the ages.

Pope Pius X declared Our Lady of Guadalupe the "Patroness of All Latin America"; Pope Pius XI, "All the Americas"; Pope Pius XII, "Empress of the Americas"; and Pope John XXIII, "The Celestial Missionary of the New World" and "The Mother of the Americas."

Prayer

Father of Mercy,

you have placed your

people in the care of

Our Lady of Guadalupe.

Through her intercession,

may we claim the dignity

of men and women created

in your likeness.

May we work for the

equality of all peoples

of the earth.

Amen.

Our Lady of the Immaculate Conception of El Viejo

Although most of the figure is covered with robes that are changed for different liturgical feasts, one can see the beautiful head of this thirty-three inch wood statue. The Virgin's gentle and modest expression, accented with dark indigenous features, faces slightly downward as she clasps her hands in prayer over her heart.

DECEMBER 8 Although historical data is limited, many speculate that this image of the Immaculate Conception was a gift from Saint Teresa of Ávila to her brother Rodrigo de Cepeda y Ahumada. According to legend, when he arrived in Nicaragua, he moved into a Franciscan mission in El Viejo, where he placed the image in a room that he converted into an oratory. When it was time for his transfer to Peru, he attempted to bring the image with him, but his ship would not sail due to persistent storms. He finally accepted that Mary wished to stay in Nicaragua, so he offered her to the people of El Viejo, and she has remained there ever since.

The image of the Immaculate Conception permeates Catholic society in Nicaragua. The liturgical feast day for this devotion—December 8—is also a national holiday. The faithful decorate their homes with altars that can be viewed from the outside, and they treat visitors with sweets and local favorite foods in anticipation of the feast of their patroness.

Pilgrims also flock to her shrine every year to polish the precious metals that have been given to her over the centuries.

Prayer

Mary Immaculate,
in you God prepared a
worthy dwelling place for
his Son and preserved you
from the stain of sin.
Awaken all Nicaraguans,
and all people,
to God's loving plan,
and grant us the courage
to embrace it with faith.
Amen.

Our Lady of Antigua

This vibrant 31 1/2-by-79-inch painting depicts the Assumption of Mary into heaven. She holds a rose in her right hand, which is a reference to the Song of Songs 2:1—"I am a rose of Sharon"—and a reminder of the second-century legend of the discovery of flowers in her tomb confirming her bodily assumption. Her blue cloak sprinkled with flowers—as opposed to the typical star motif—further confirms her complete passage into heaven. She holds Jesus in her left arm while two angels greet her with a golden crown.

AUGUST 15 The roots of this devotion date back to the beginning of the sixteenth century in Spain and the reconstruction of the Cathedral of Seville where all but one wall was replaced. The painting of Our Lady's Assumption remained on this wall, and thus it became known as *Santa Maria de la Antigua*, literally, "Holy Mary of the Ancient (*Antiqua*) Cathedral."

The devotion traveled to Panama in 1510, when Spaniards promised the Virgin that if they survived a battle against the indigenous, they would name a town after her. And so it happened that a city—and later the church—was named Santa Maria de la Antigua.

Shortly thereafter, Pope Leo X (1513) created the first diocese in Panama at Santa Maria de la Antigua, and the church built in Our Lady's honor was named its cathedral. When Panama City was founded and named capital in 1519, the seat of the diocese was transferred to it, and the image of Our Lady became its patroness. During the jubilee year of 2000, she was proclaimed the patron saint of Panama during a ceremony that consecrated the nation to the Immaculate Heart of Mary.

Prayer

Queen of Heaven

and Earth,

the people of Panama

have long looked

to you for strength.

With them,

we ask you

to remain with all your

Son's faithful people

and never let us doubt

your motherly love.

Amen.

Our Lady of the Miracles of Caacupé

Our Lady of Caacupé is a representation of the Immaculate Conception of Mary. As usual, her hands are folded in prayer while she stands crushing a serpent—signs of her defeat over sin—on top of the earth and half moon. She wears a beautiful white tunic and blue cloak, each laced with golden edges, as symbols of her divine sanction. This powerful image, complete with delicate facial features, blond hair, and a golden crown, is only twenty inches tall.

DECEMBER 8 Our Lady of Caacupé emerged during the early part of the sixteenth century, when the Mbayáes tribe rejected Christianity and declared war on all converts. During one of their attacks, a converted Indian from a Franciscan mission sought refuse behind a massive tree. Trembling in fear, he prayed to the Immaculate Mary and promised her that if he survived, he would carve an image of her from the trunk of the tree that shielded him. The young Indian avoided death and carved two images of Our Lady: one for the local church and another for his own devotion.

Many years later a great flood threatened to destroy the region near the Franciscan mission. The local faithful once again placed their trust in the Immaculate Mary. They were spared and from then on named the image "Virgin of Miracles."

Considered to be the religious center of Paraguay, the present church was constructed in 1945, and was declared the Sanctuary of the Virgin of the Miracles of Caacupé in 1980. On December 8 pilgrims flock to the Virgin's sanctuary to offer prayers of thanks and praise for Our Lady's role in their Christian identity.

Prayer

Blessed Mother,

the people of Paraguay

venerate you

under the title

Our Lady of the Miracles.

Through your guidance,

they have found

protection and life.

Never fail to assist

our efforts to protect and

promote all human life.

Amen.

Our Lady of Mercy

The Virgin appears as she did to the founder of the Mercedarian Order in the thirteenth century: wearing a white tunic which has a long scapular that bears the shield of the Order at her breast. A cloak covers her shoulders and outstretched hands which hold a royal scepter in her right hand and open chains in her left hand (symbols of liberation from Moslem captivity).

SEPTEMBER 24 According to tradition, the image of Our Lady of Mercy first appeared to Saint Peter Nolasco and James I, King of Aragon and Catalonia, in 1218 during separate visions which requested them to found an order dedicated to rescuing Christians from Moslem persecution. Shortly thereafter, the Order of Our Lady of Mercy (Mercedarian Order) was founded and approved in 1235 by Pope Gregory IX.

In the sixteenth century the friars spread to Peru and by 1535 they built a primitive chapel that served as the first Christian parish. They built a permanent church in 1540, and they continued to evangelize the city and assist with the development of its infrastructure and cultural heritage. The significance of their work eventually spread throughout the country, and the church and statue of Our Lady became national symbols.

In 1730 Our Lady was declared the "Patroness of the Peruvian Lands," and in 1823 the "Patroness of the Armies of the Republic." On September 24, 1924, during the ceremony honoring the first centennial of the nations independence (July 28, 1824), the statue was solemnly crowned and the Feast of Our Lady of Mercy was declared a national holiday.

Prayer

Our Lady of Mercy,

you are close to all people

in their sufferings.

With your help,

may the women

and men of Peru,

and all your Son's followers,

be signs of hope

in times of

darkness and violence.

Amen.

Our Lady of Divine Providence

Based on a thirteenth-century oil painting, the statue portrays the Child Jesus sleeping across the lap of the seated Virgin. Her folded hands support the left hand of the Child, and together they pray with tenderness for the people of Puerto Rico. The white-and-blue decoration of this woodcarving emulates traditional Marian imagery.

NOVEMBER 19 Devotion to Our Lady of Divine Providence originated in Italy during the thirteenth century and spread rapidly to Spain, where a shrine was erected and became the center through which devotion was to spread around the world .

In 1853 a bishop from Catalonia was named the ordinary of Puerto Rico, and thus the devotion was born on the island. When he arrived, he found the diocese in physical and financial peril. He placed the diocese into the hands of Divine Providence, and in less than five years the physical strength of the diocese mirrored the strong faith of the people. In honor of her assistance, the faithful accepted Our Lady into their worship and way of living.

In 1969 Pope Paul VI declared Our Lady of Divine Providence the principal patroness of the island of Puerto Rico. He also transferred the Virgin's solemnity from January 2 to November 19 in order to align the people's affection for Our Lady with the day of the island's discovery.

Prayer

Mother of

Divine Providence,

to the hungry you have

provided food,

to the imprisoned you have

offered consolation,

and to the downtrodden

you have offered liberation.

Help us bring to others

the freedom won by

Christ's sacrifice.

Amen.

Our Lady of Thirty-Three Patriots

This baroque woodcarving of the Assumption of Mary is only thirty-three inches tall. The Virgin holds her hands in prayer, while the motion of her blue-and-white cloak allude to her heavenly ascent. She stands on a half moon and globe which are supported by a cloud and three angels. The disproportionate size of her golden crown has become the distinctive feature of this portrayal of Mary.

SECOND SUNDAY OF NOVEMBER

The statue of Our Lady of Thirty-Three Patriots originated with the eighteenth century Jesuit missions in Paraguay. The Guarani workshops flourished among these missions, and it is assumed that they were responsible for this image. It was first used in 1779 in a small Jesuit chapel in the village of Pintado before being moved, along with all the residents, to the city of Florida, where it remained for many years as the object of veneration.

In April 1825, thirty-three Uruguayan patriots landed on the beaches of Agraciada to begin the war for independence, and they placed the struggles of their emerging nation under the protection of Mary. When they arrived in Florida, they formally consecrated the fate of their nation to Mary at the feet of the statue. Four months later they achieved national independence, and from that day forward the statue was referred to as Our Lady of the Thirty-Three Patriots.

Pope John XXIII crowned the image in 1961, and he officially proclaimed her the "Patroness of Uruguay."

Prayer

Loving Mother,

at a crucial moment

in Uruguay's history,

you inspired the thirty-

three patriots to ask God's

assistance in their

pursuit of freedom.

Grant courage to all your

sons and daughters

committed to the

pursuit of freedom.

Amen.

Our Lady of Coromoto

This is one of several statues that depict Our Lady of Coromoto as she appeared on a small piece of parchment to an Indian chief. The Virgin is seated with the Child Jesus on her lap. Both look outward with royal crowns upon their heads. Mary wears a rich crimson cloak, white veil, and straw-colored tunic. The original 1½-by-1-inch holy card is enshrined in the pedestal of the throne.

SEPTEMBER 11 When the Spanish settlers arrived in the region of Guanare around 1591, the Coromoto Indians abandoned their land to avoid conversion to Christianity.

Sixty years later the chief of the Coromoto tribe experienced a vision of Our Lady upon the waters of the Tucupido River. She summoned him to go to the settlers to receive the healing waters of Christian baptism.

The chief tried to convert, but he could not adjust to the new way of life, and he returned to his village with his family. Our Lady appeared to him again, but the chief was annoyed and he struck out at the Virgin. As he attempted to catch her, she disappeared and left a small holy card in his clenched fist bearing her image. The small parchment was placed into the church at Guanare, where it was preserved in a reliquary until 1987, when it was placed into the pedestal of the wooden statue of Our Lady of Coromoto.

Pope Pius XII declared this image the "Patroness of the Republic of Venezuela," and he elevated the church that holds it to the status of basilica in 1949. A second shrine was built on the site of the second apparition and inaugurated with a Solemn Mass celebrated by Pope John Paul II in 1996.

Prayer

Blessed Mother,

from the beginning of

Venezuela's history you

have afforded your people

protection and encouraged

them to pursue freedom.

May we recognize the

dignity of all men

and women,

and work together for the

coming of the kingdom

promised by Jesus.

Amen.